Hurt Sounds

New Women's Voices Series, No. 185

poems by

Isabella J Mansfield

Finishing Line Press
Georgetown, Kentucky

Hurt Sounds

New Women's Voices Series, No. 185

Publisher: Leah Huete de Maines
Editor: Christen Kincaid
Cover Art: Pete Mundt
Author Photo: Ryan Rupprecht
Cover Design: Isabella J Mansfield

Order online: www.finishinglinepress.com
also available on amazon.com

Author inquiries and mail orders:
Finishing Line Press
PO Box 1626
Georgetown, Kentucky 40324
USA

Contents

For Dad

"and if you should say goodbye, I'll still go on loving you."
—Dion and The Belmonts

Content Warning

the poems in this book relate to parental death and grief

please be kind to yourself, today and always

Pecan Pie

my dad made the
best pecan pie
—or so I am told—
I never tried it.
I don't remember
many Thanksgivings
with him at home.
Divorce has a way
of separating you
from the things
you didn't know
you were missing.

Bukowski Wrote

Bukowski wrote a lot about whiskey.
I did too, for a while.

Truth is, I never really drank
that much.

Knowing I would forget everything
is why I stopped.

Knowing I would forget everything
is why I started.

Windows

they have replaced the windows
of this historic building

the old hotel

they were leaking and they stuck;
some of the cranks were broken

some no longer opened at all

the built-in blinds were yellowed with age
but provided a cavern-like feel

it was always dark

they blocked the sun in such a way that you never
noticed the dust motes hanging in the air

everything seemed suspended in time

they have replaced the windows entirely
down to the framework

they didn't notice

the walls are also cracked and damaged;
there are water stains

layers of neglect

the transparency of these new windows
without their blinds is a shock to the eye

the whole world can see inside

there is nowhere now to hide from the sun
and the dust as it settles

Hey Dad

I tuned your guitar
for you

I had hoped
you would play

I understand
your fingers

don't have
the strength

but watching
you try, then

give up
tugs my

heartstrings
out of tune

Senryu Trio for Dad

watching my father
fall apart requires a
strength I do not have

he holds an unlit
cigarette out of habit
to his downturned mouth

they do not allow
smoking here but he asks for
a light anyway

Some Years Are Like That

some years
it snows early
for a long time

and everything becomes
padded, silenced
I swear in those moments

if you stand still long enough

you can feel the Earth slow down
just a little, feel the whirring
of snowfall around your cheeks

some years though
some years the ice is so thick
it loses its transparency

the air steals the breath
from your lungs
and redistributes it

Accidental Eulogy

I accidentally wrote a eulogy for my father.
He has not died, but the man I knew
is gone

"Hello my daughter," he used to say,
"my little liebchen," a nod to German heritage
I never knew

Sundays were for phone calls and summers
were spent watching baseball or fishing
for Bluegill

I still know the feeling of his arm as a makeshift
seatbelt at the stoplight, in case the manufacturer's
failed to hold

I let his stubble scratch my fingers, drew him
with a mustache and later, without, but always
with his glasses

He only took me to places I wanted to go,
always bought me ice cream, and never stole
my french fries

We would sing for what felt like hours, play
at my favorite park and I would draw quietly
when he took a nap

He used to clean offices; I loved the face he made
when he'd say the word "squeegee," sometimes
he'd let me clean his window, too

He smoked too much, drank too much,
never around me. He was overprotective
though only a part-time parent

And yet, his love for me was constant
even now, in the long shadows, he greets me:
"Hello my daughter, my little *liebchen*."

How To Leave Home

(inspired by the 1954 "Vacationer's Checklist," Henry Ford Museum, Dearborn MI)

First of all
stop the milk
before it spoils
on your porch
and the paper
            you will not need
            the news where
            you are going
the laundry can wait
leave a key with a neighbor
            but empty your icebox
                        and lower the thermostat
please remember to
turn off the lights
when you leave
hold your mail
you do not want
to issue open invitations
for burglars and don't
            forget to notify
the police of your absence
            they do not have better
                        things to do than watch
                                    your empty home

I Don't Hear God

when i pray I am
only reciting someone
else's poetry

Dad Wait

you were supposed to wake up
and tell me where you liked to fish
on the Fox River
or the Kalamazoo River
the rivers are long and I don't
know which spot was
better for fishing or where
you just like the scenery
the rivers are new rivers now
so I guess it doesn't matter
if I stand where you stood
the water isn't the same water
and the rocks aren't the same rocks
but I would stand there anyway
and let the fish swim around my feet
wondering if they were the daughters of
fish who swam around your feet, too

How Final the Room (Where You Died)

I can't forget how final the silence
of your room, how empty, after
both you and the nurse left;
how it was just us, but just me.

I am told even those afraid of death
find comfort at the bedside
of a loved one, but I felt only small;
shrank and backed away to the window.

In a nightmare, I'd have climbed through
the glass to get away, if we had not
been on the fourth floor
of the hospital, pulled down

by the gravity of grief and terror
and shame, at fearing the thing
in your bed that looked like you
but was not, could not be you again.

Were you scared? Or was your grip
on life as weak as the last time you
held your guitar, fingers barely
making contact; unsure, unfamiliar.

In the days I had with you, I read.
I played music for you. I sang.
I watched the world burn around me.
I wondered what you thought of it all.

I have entered a year that
will never have you in it,
a year untouched by your impression.
All the years forward, without.

I wonder if you knew I was there,
and if you did, did you know I was scared,
and if you did, what would you have said
to my fear. What should I have said?

How final the room, how full
of silence. What is the next part?
What do I say when I go? How do I leave?
How heavy the door, how quiet the latch.

The Mahogany Box

sits, just out of the way,
on the tile in front of our fireplace
(if this is ironic in some way, it is unintentional)

I left it in the box it shipped in for a week
until I could no longer stand to read the words
"Cremated Remains" on all sides

I don't know what to do with my father's ashes
and every day that passes since his death
feels like time wasted

I should plan a memorial but I don't know how
I don't want my dad to be referred to
in past tense

some days I say hello to the box, press
my hand to the top the way he used to rest
his hand on my knee

some days I lay awake and am afraid of my
living room, I cannot understand how my dad
fits in a box I can carry

I worry that I am not grieving correctly
I don't want him to be disappointed
in me even now

he used to say he would follow me anywhere
would always be there for me, no matter the distance,
no matter how far

they tell me he is always with me now but
that's just the thing you say to the grieving, he
feels farther away than ever

if, one day, I scatter the ashes, bury them or
whatever it is I am supposed to do,
what then, do I do with an empty box?

Do They Play the Blues in Heaven?

I remember every note
he ever played for me
every song we sang together
he would belt the blues and I never
understood the lyrics
his stories told
with guitar strings.
I never let him teach me
how to play
I wonder if his guitar
would remember me
and if she would sing
to my poems the way
he would sing
to me

When the Phone Doesn't Ring

it feels like you forgot my birthday
this year and the two years before that
this year, you didn't call
you won't
you can't
so I replay the last message you left me
it is three years old now
and only fourteen seconds long
I can't remember but I hope
I called you back
I hope I told you I loved you
I know that you did

thank you for calling

I Had the Date Wrong

I thought I had two more days
before I'd be forced to remember
the way your last breath rattled
as it circled your throat.

It has been two years
and I still cannot
bring myself to open
your guitar case.

I have been unable to plot
a memorial or a location
for the urn, where your ashes
have settled on its side.

I thought I had more time
to steel myself against
memory before the swell
of grief filled my throat.

This year, your rose bush
is slow to bloom; purple leaves
unfurling in June, as if to say
"I thought I had more time."

Guitar Case

the inside of your
guitar case still smells like you.
When I touch these strings
its like holding your hand and
I hear your voice resonate

On the Anniversary

of my father's death, we put
a fish into the ground. This is not

some three-years-gone,
Dad-loved-to-fish

symbolism. It is instead
poor timing or a cruel joke

from the universe.
The death of a beloved pet

days before, and the only day
that worked for a burial

happened to be Sunday,
the fourth of June.

The third year after my dad
would never go fishing

ever again and the first time
my son never wanted

to love a new pet ever again,
having now experienced

sharp grief in his chest,
salt-stiffened skin on his cheeks

and the heft of loss
in his belly.

Acknowledgments

If I'd had any say, this would be a different book, one that didn't revolve around the passing of my father. In 2019, he told me he wasn't at all surprised that I'd become a successful writer. One year later, he was gone. He never had the chance to see me read my own work in a bookstore, I never had the chance to tell him how many weeks my books sat on the Best Seller shelf. To my "Crabby Old Daddy," I love you and miss you more than any blues song could express.

To my husband, Matt, and our son, Travis. I am so glad you're mine. Thank you for sharing me with bookstores, stages, and other poets, and for always being the home I return to.

To my families: my work family, my friends, and of course, my mom, siblings, and too many nieces and nephews to list. Thank you for seeing and loving me because of who I am (and not in spite of it!)

My love also to my Poetry Family—those I've shared space with, written with, laughed with, and cried with, especially the open mic and workshop regulars. You make me a better poet, and poetry makes a better world. Keep going.

To Jeri Kay, Jeanne, Kelly, Ethan, Mia, Anne, Phil, Chuck and all of the staff (plus Luna and Myrtle of course!) at 2 Dandelions Bookshop in Brighton, MI. What would I do without my favorite bookstore, my home-base. Thank you for sharing your space and your readers, your hearts and your friendship. So much of my success and support, I owe to you. I simply cannot imagine a world without Dandelions.

Several poems have been previously published, and I would like to extend my most sincere thanks to the editors for seeing and publishing my work.

Some Years Are Like That, *Capsule Stories "Bare Bones,"* 09/2020

Windows, *East Jasmine Review "Tell Me More" Anthology,* 11/2020

How Final The Room (Where You Died), *Bitchin' Kitsch/All My Relations,* 02/2021

Do They Play the Blues in Heaven? (Honorable Mention and publication) *Poetry Society of Michigan/Peninsula Poets Contest and anthology* 07/2024

Author of six chapbooks, **Isabella J Mansfield** (she/her) is an award-winning and internationally acclaimed poet. Known as much for her charismatic and powerful poetry readings as she is her deeply personal poems, Mansfield's work shines a light on depression and anxiety, intimacy, grief, physical and mental health, and disability issues. A three-time Pushcart Prize nominee, three-time Best of the Net Nominee, Write Bloody McCarthy Prize Honorable Mention, and Ritzenhein Emerging Author Award Winner, Isabella is always looking for ways to bring a little humor into her poetry and is almost never sorry to make you cry. She lives in Michigan with her husband and son.

Instagram and Facebook @isabellajmansfield

www.ingramcontent.com/pod-product-compliance
Lightning Source LLC
Chambersburg PA
CBHW022102080426
42734CB00009B/1454